Rivers

Jane & Steve Parker

Consultant: Keith Lye

FRANKLIN WATTS
NEW YORK • LONDON • SYDNEY

First published in 1997 by Franklin Watts
96 Leonard Street, London EC2A 4RH

Franklin Watts Australia, 14 Mars Road
Lane Cove, NSW 2066

© Franklin Watts 1997

Series editor: Kyla Barber
Art director: Robert Walster
Designer: Ness Wood
Illustrator: Joanna Biggs
Picture researcher: Susan Mennell
Consultant: Keith Lye

A CIP catalogue record for this book
is available from the British Library

ISBN 0 7496 2733 6

Dewey Classification 551.48

Printed in Great Britain

Contents

What are Rivers? 4

The River Begins 6

Rivers Shape the Land 8

White Waters 10

Slow and Sedate 12

Into the Sea 14

River Plants 16

Animals of the River 18

Spirits of the River 20

Water of Life 22

Floating Down the Highway 24

Factories and Industries 26

Preserving Rivers 28

Glossary 30

Fact File 31

Index 32

What are Rivers?

Rivers are fascinating, exciting, beautiful and endlessly varied. They spray and tumble down steep hillsides, thunder and foam over giant waterfalls, glide slowly and silently through the countryside, teem with fish and birds, and bustle with ships and boats in our cities and ports.

Mighty Amazon

Rivers cross the landscapes around the world. They carry fresh water from the highlands, across the plains and eventually out to sea.

Mightiest river of all is the Amazon in South America. It carries 60 times as much water as the Nile, the world's longest river. The area that a river's water collects from is its basin. The Amazon basin covers nearly one-twentieth of the Earth's land surface.

The Amazon and its tributaries wander and meander through tropical forest, before they join and head out to sea.

Snow and rain

The Amazon begins as melting snow on the Andes Mountains, in western South America. It drips and dribbles over rocks and through soil, gathering into small streams and brooks. These join to form larger branches, or tributaries, that feed into the main channel of the great Amazon itself, which continues to grow as it collects the rainwater that pours down on its great tropical forests.

Approximate lengths in kilometres: **Nile** (world's longest) 6,670; **Amazon** (world's biggest) 6,450

FIVE WORLD RIVERS

ARCTIC OCEAN

GREENLAND

RUSSIA

CANADA

EUROPE

CHINA ← **HUANG HE**

USA

INDIA

MISSISSIPPI

AFRICA

GANGES

AMAZON

NILE

N
W ⊕ E
S

BRAZIL

AUSTRALIA

ANTARCTIC OCEAN

ANTARCTICA

Take 5 rivers

Amazon (South America) is the world's largest river and is home to the world's richest wildlife – in the river itself and in the surrounding lakes, swamps and forests.

Nile (North-east Africa) is longer than the Amazon, but carries less water. It flows through parched deserts, past the huge pyramids built thousands of years ago by the Ancient Egyptians.

Mississippi (USA) is the "Big Muddy"; slow, wide and cloudy in its lower course. It was one of the world's busiest waterways, thronged with paddle-steamers and barges.

Ganges (India) is considered sacred by Hindus. It provides water for cooking, washing and farming, but is threatened by increasing levels of pollution.

Huang He, formerly called **Hwang Ho** (China), yellow with silt, it waters farmland that feeds over 100 million people.

Rivers on Mars?

Around 1900, American astronomer Percival Lowell studied the planet Mars through his telescope. He thought he saw criss-cross patterns of straight canals, built by intelligent beings. The legend of Martians began. Today we know, from spacecraft pictures, that Lowell was wrong. But deep grooves in the rocky surface and wide fan-like areas of sand show that Mars probably had water, long ago. It flowed not in constructed canals, but in natural river channels.

River channels and cliffs on Mars.

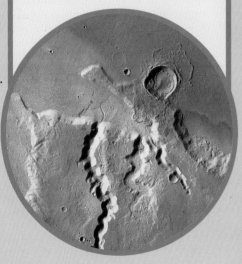

Huang He 4,830; **Mississippi** 3,800; and **Ganges** 2,507.

5

The River Begins

The weak afternoon sun shines into an icy cave near Nanda Devi, high in the Himalaya Mountains. As temperatures creep above freezing, ice melts and dribbles over rocks into a stream that flows from the mouth of the cave. This is the tiny beginning of the great Ganges, sacred river of the Hindu faith.

The "Cow's Mouth", the ice-cave source of the Ganges, 4,000 metres high in the Himalayas.

Joining together

A river's smallest, earliest stages are called first-order streams. The Ganges has thousands of them. Like any flowing water, they follow the steepest path downhill that they can find, trickling and bubbling and joining into larger, second-order streams, and so on, and on.

Bigger and bigger

As the brooks and streams merge and enlarge, they eventually form a young river. In the Ganges' case, this is the Alaknanda. Still falling steeply through the Himalayan valleys, it meets another river, the Bhagirathi. These are two of the main tributaries, or branches, of the Ganges.

A boulder worn smooth by centuries of rushing water.

River sources: **Nile:** Great Lakes of East Africa; **Amazon:** high in the Peruvian Andes;

Across India

The Ganges flows east across India, along the Himalayan foothills (lower slopes). It is swollen by dozens more tributaries, fed by melting snow on the peaks, and upland rain. It forms part of the India-Bangladesh border, then sweeps across the low plains of Bangladesh.

Mountain ranges are the source of many major rivers. The Indus, like the Ganges, begins in the Himalayas and is fed by snowfall on the high peaks.

Two-thirds of river water comes from snow or rain. The rest oozes or bubbles from the rocks and ground, as springs.

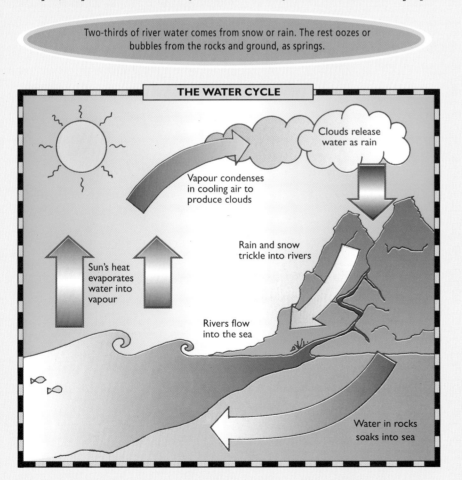

THE WATER CYCLE

Clouds release water as rain

Vapour condenses in cooling air to produce clouds

Rain and snow trickle into rivers

Sun's heat evaporates water into vapour

Rivers flow into the sea

Water in rocks soaks into sea

A hidden source

The Orinoco flows for about 2,500 kilometres, mainly through rainforests and pampas (grasslands) in Venezuela and Colombia (northern South America). Its massive muddy mouth or delta, over 20,000 square kilometres, was one of the first sights seen by sailor and explorer Christopher Columbus in 1498, on his third voyage to the American continent. Despite expeditions in 1560 and 1799, the river's source was only found in 1951, high in the Andes Mountains.

The Orinoco meanders through thick rainforest, depositing banks of sand in the slower sections.

Mississippi: Lake Itasca, Minnesota; **Ganges:** Nanda Devi, Himalayas; **Huang He:** Tibetan Plateau.

Rivers Shape the Land

Rivers usually start on high ground, where there is plenty of rain or snow. They are steep and fast at first, rushing down the mountains and hillsides. Then they flow more slowly across the flatter plains, towards the sea.

Some streams are fed by melting glaciers, "rivers of ice".

River valleys

Fast-flowing river water picks up stones and bits of rock which frost action has broken off the peaks. These bounce and grind against the river bed, knocking off more pieces. This wearing-away is called erosion. Gradually the river erodes deeper into the rock. If the underlying rock is very hard and the river is fast, it may form a deep gorge or canyon with steep sides.

Lower down, the slopes get shallower and the water moves more slowly. This means smaller rocky pieces, like pebbles and gravel, settle onto the bottom. The river has less force to cut a straight path, or course. So it meanders (winds) gently to create curving valleys.

A young, fast river can move great boulders.

Height of source area above sea level, in metres: **Ganges:** over 4,000 metres;

Erosion and formation

Constant erosion means that rivers wear away mountains and uplands. They carry, or transport, rocks and soil to the lowlands and finally into the seas. Over millions of years, the smaller pieces settle out as layers of sediments. As the sediments deepen, the lowest ones are squashed and cemented into solid rock by the weight of the layers above. So the mountains get lower and the sea bed gets higher.

But the Earth is restless. Massive movements crumple and buckle the sea bed, lifting it up to form mountains. And the whole process starts again! This never-ending cycle of rock erosion and formation has been happening since the Earth formed, with rivers playing a vital part in shaping the landscape.

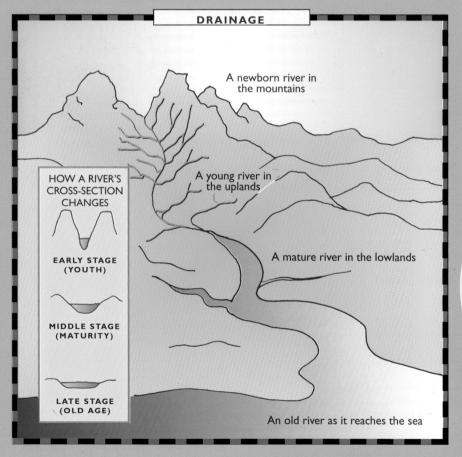

DRAINAGE

A newborn river in the mountains

A young river in the uplands

A mature river in the lowlands

An old river as it reaches the sea

HOW A RIVER'S CROSS-SECTION CHANGES

EARLY STAGE (YOUTH)

MIDDLE STAGE (MATURITY)

LATE STAGE (OLD AGE)

Amazon and **Huang He:** over 2,000; **Nile:** about 1,500; **Mississippi:** less than 500.

White Waters

Water follows the steepest and straightest course, often within a channel. But sometimes, when the rocks are hard, the water spreads out over a wider, shallower course. But the same volume of water must still pass, so the river speeds up and forms fast, foamy-white shallows, raging rapids or even bigger cataracts.

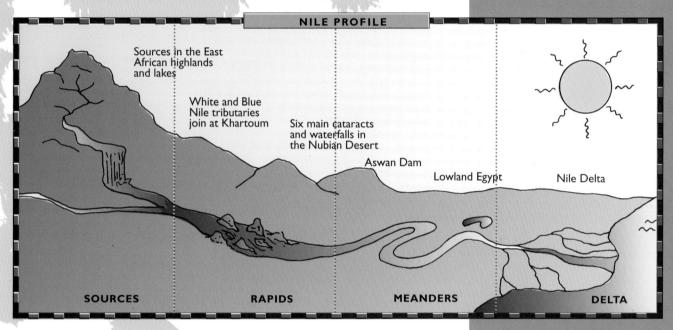

NILE PROFILE

Sources in the East African highlands and lakes

White and Blue Nile tributaries join at Khartoum

Six main cataracts and waterfalls in the Nubian Desert

Aswan Dam

Lowland Egypt

Nile Delta

SOURCES

RAPIDS

MEANDERS

DELTA

The Nile's cataracts are between its upland sources and its lowland meanders.

Six stretches of solid stone

As the River Nile crosses the Nubian Desert in northern Africa, it flows over six stretches of hard granite rock. The water tumbles over them in short, fast hops. These shallow, fast-flowing, rocky, dangerous parts of rivers are called cataracts or, on smaller rivers, rapids. Like so many river features, they depend on the hardness of the underlying rock, the angle of its slope and the amount of water flowing over it.

Steepest slopes: In places, the **Nile** cataracts descend at 1 metre per 50 metres.

Waterfalls

Far upstream, the Nile is formed by two tributaries, the White and Blue Niles. Millions of years ago, the White Nile was almost blocked as Earth movements threw up a wall of very hard rock across its path. The water built up behind, and thundered over the lowest part of the rim as a waterfall.

At waterfalls like the Caracol Falls, Brazil, a river plunges over a hard rim, or lip, of rock. It wears away a deep hole below.

Moving upstream

The plunging cascade of a waterfall relentlessly wears away the softer rock of the river bed. This eats its way under the hard rim, forming a lip or overhang. Finally the lip collapses and the waterfall suddenly moves upstream, leaving a gorge in its place.

Niagara

The Niagara River, between Canada and the USA, carries water from Lake Erie to Lake Ontario, which is 99 metres lower. Over 50 metres of the drop is Niagara Falls. The spectacular torrent thunders over hard surface rocks, undercutting the softer shale and limestone rocks beneath. There are two parts of the falls divided by an island – the American Falls (305 metres wide) and the Horseshoe or Canadian Falls (790 metres wide).

The raging torrent of Niagara's Horseshoe Falls dwarfs the *Maid of the Mist* pleasure boat with its spray-soaked tourists.

Huang He runs downhill at more than 1 metre per 500 metres in its upper reaches.

Slow and Sedate

As a river leaves the slopes of the foothills, and begins its journey across flatter ground, it is said to become older or "mature". The river now has less energy to cut its course so the water flows slowly and steadily, along gently sloping valleys and across wide plains.

Yellow silt

The Huang He River, which begins in the Tibetan Plateau of China, flows sedately across northern China. It is known as the Yellow River because it picks up yellow-tinged mud and silt from an upland area in north-west China. The river carries so much yellow silt that the sea it flows into is called the Yellow Sea.

The Huang He's waters, laden with bright yellow silt.

Devastating floods

The Huang He has another name – "Sorrow of China". It brings water to 100 million people but it also causes devastating floods. As the river crosses the North China Plain, it flows between silt banks, or levées. Its surface is up to 10 metres above the surrounding land. If the river breaks these banks during the rainy season, it swamps and smothers nearby villages and farms in thick, sticky mud.

The worst flood disaster on record was in 1887, when the Huang He burst its banks and 900,000 people died.

Approximate size of drainage basin in square kilometres: **Amazon:** more than 7 million;

This river in Cambodia, South-east Asia, is brown with silt as it winds its way through the flat countryside. The river is in its mature stage.

Changing course

Mature rivers tend to wander and change their course over the flat plains. The Huang He has done this twenty-six times in China's long recorded history. One type of change is an ox-bow, shown below, formed when a meander becomes more and more curved. Finally the river breaks through the narrow "waist" and flows straight again, leaving the bend as an isolated ox-bow lake. In Australia, these types of lake are called billabongs, an Aboriginal name meaning "dead water".

Summer flooding

The Brahmaputra is a major river in India and Bangladesh. It flows past the Shillong Plateau, one of India's wettest areas, where 20 metres of rain can fall in the summer season. This makes the river rise up to 12 metres above its normal level. The floodwaters may cover an 8-kilometre wide area of land, killing people and destroying homes and farms.

Rivers in flood can drown farmland, roads and villages.

MEANDER TO OX-BOW

Sand and mud bars added on inner curve

Bank eaten away on outer curve

River cuts through narrow "waist"

Old river course becomes ox-bow lake

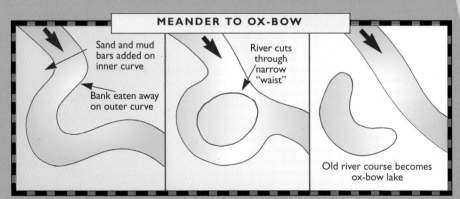

At a river's bend, slower water on the inner curve drops sediments to form sand and mud bars. Faster water on the outer curve cuts away the bank. Gradually the meander gets more curved and is finally cut off.

Nile: 3.35 million; **Mississippi:** 3.25 million; **Ganges:** 1.03 million; **Huang He:** 0.75 million.

Into the Sea

Not all rivers flow into the sea. In south-west Africa, the Okavango River spreads out, dribbles and drains away into the hot sands of the Kalahari Desert. But for most rivers, their final destination is a sea or an ocean. At the river's mouth, fresh water pours into and mixes with the salty seawater. Its flow slows, and the last of its sediment settles onto the bottom – the finest, lightest particles of mud and silt.

Estuaries

The type of river mouth depends partly on the sea currents in the area. If they continually sweep away the river's sediment, the mouth stays clear and is called an estuary. The Amazon River forms an estuary. The muddy estuary bed is submerged by the river's outgoing fresh water at low tide, and the sea's incoming salt water at high tide.

As seen from space, the grey Nile Delta muds separate desert and blue sea.

Deltas

Along some coasts, sediment is dumped at the river's mouth to form large flat areas, swampy islands and sand banks. These areas of land are called deltas.

Some deltas are triangular in shape. Some of them, called arcuate deltas, have curved, or arc-like edges. Others, called bird's-foot deltas, form when the sediment piles up along a river's banks. The banks create long fingers of land that jut out into the sea.

The **Amazon** estuary is 240 kilometres wide; the **Mississippi** has a bird's-foot delta;

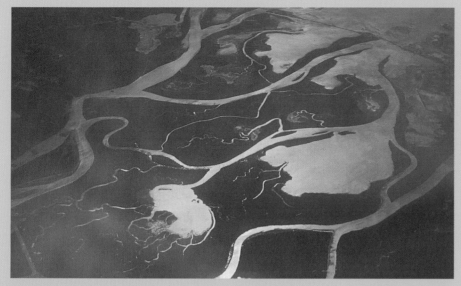

The Mississippi Delta has hundreds of endlessly shifting channels and pools.

The delta of the Ganges-Brahmaputra, on the India-Bangladesh border, covers 75,000 square kilometres – more than half the size of England.

Growing fast

Every year, the Mississippi Delta creeps another 90 metres into the Gulf of Mexico, laying down half a billion tonnes of silt. About half a million years ago, this river was almost 1,000 kilometres shorter.

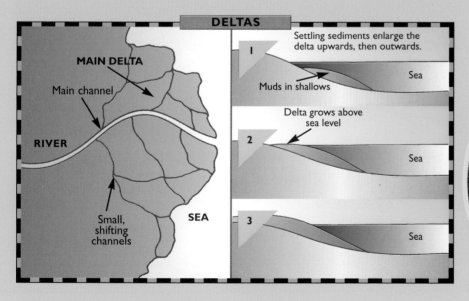

DELTAS

MAIN DELTA

Main channel

RIVER

Small, shifting channels

SEA

Settling sediments enlarge the delta upwards, then outwards.

1

Sea

Muds in shallows

Delta grows above sea level

2

Sea

3

Sea

Holding back the flood

In south-east England, the River Thames flows into the sea through its estuary. Twice each day, high tides make sea water surge about 12 kilometres upstream. If a high tide meets flood waters coming downstream, after heavy rain, the river could break its banks – and flood London. In 1982 the Thames Flood Barrier was completed at Woolwich, east London. Massive semicircular gates lie on the river bed, between huge piers. When floods threaten, the gates swivel upwards to hold back the rising tide.

The closed Thames Barrier.

The **Nile, Ganges** and **Huang He** have arcuate deltas. The **Huang He's** grows 2 km each year.

River Plants

Rivers are ideal places for plants. There's a constant supply of their most essential substance, water. However, if the current is too rapid, few plants can stay anchored. They are swept away in the torrent. Fast streams and rivers are mainly vegetated by mosses and ferns on the spray-splashed bankside.

A need for light

River water brings many nutrients for plant food, such as minerals soaking through the surrounding soil, and bits of rotting debris. But plants also need light for growth. So they thrive where there are no steep gorges, overhanging rocks or shady trees. They flourish even more on the unshaded banks of slower rivers, at the surface, and in the shallow, clearer waters.

Papyrus reeds and rushes love the wet warmth of tropical riverbanks.

In one growing season, ten water hyacinths can multiply to two million, covering two soccer pitches.

Along the banks

The world's greatest variety of plants and animals live in the tropical rainforests of the Amazon and its tributaries. The forest floor is laced with millions of tiny streams that carry water into the mighty river. Ferns and mosses grow in abundance. The tall forest trees drop their seeds into the river, to float away and find new places to grow – even across the sea.

Well-known plants: **Amazon:** giant water lilies; **Nile:** papyrus;

You could walk on Amazon giant water lily leaves, like stepping stones.

At the water's edge

The plants change as the water deepens. Reeds, rushes and sedges, with their thick and matted roots, like marshy shallows. Water-weeds live slightly deeper, waving in the current. Water lilies have stems more than three metres long, so their roots are buried in the nutritious river bed mud, while their leaves and flowers float on the surface.

Beautiful danger

In their natural Amazon home, water hyacinths are kept in balance by other plants and animals. But in the late 1800s, they were taken to other regions, such as North America and Africa, to decorate garden ponds with their beautiful flowers. Without natural controls, they multiplied and spread. Now water hyacinths are the world's number one water-weed. They block waterways and smother fish and other wildlife in over fifty tropical countries.

This aerial view shows water hyacinths clogging vast areas of the Nile in Africa. They upset the balance of wildlife and block boats.

PLANT ZONES

Plants thrive in different zones, from dry bank to the river's middle.

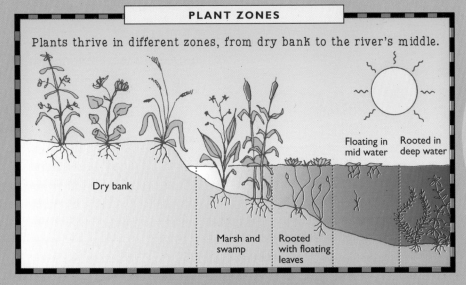

Dry bank

Marsh and swamp

Rooted with floating leaves

Floating in mid water

Rooted in deep water

Mississippi: swamp cypress; **Ganges:** lotus; **Huǎng He:** water chestnut.

Animals of the River

We rarely see the fish, shellfish and other animals that live in rivers. But they are just as varied as creatures living along the banks. Their watery homes vary from cold, clear, rushing torrents on high hills, to slow, warm, muddy waters in tropical forests.

Salmon leap waterfalls to reach their cool, clear breeding streams.

Cool water

The Nile's upland tributaries are cool, clear and fast. Water shrimps, snails, and insect larvae (young) such as stoneflies shelter under pebbles and cling to the gravelly bottom, grabbing whatever food floats past. Birds bob about, pecking up these small creatures.

Hippos wallow in many African rivers, emerging at night to eat plants along the banks.

Well-known animals: **Amazon:** anaconda and river dolphin; **Nile:** Nile crocodile:

Above and below

Farther downstream, in slower water, shellfish and worms lie buried in the Nile's muddy bed. The Nile perch, two metres long, preys on smaller fish, frogs and water-shrews. Herons wade in the shallows and fish-eagles circle overhead.

River reptiles

The Nile soft-shelled turtle, nearly a metre long, feeds on mud-living creatures. Another reptile, the Nile crocodile, lurks near the bank and grabs water buffaloes, antelopes and similar large victims. Yet even the mighty crocodile has an enemy. Baby crocodiles are eaten by yet another reptile – the Nile monitor lizard. It swims well and chases African swamp rats when they dive into the water for safety.

The gharial (or gavial) is a type of fish-eating crocodile from the Ganges and nearby rivers.

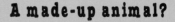

A made-up animal?

A platypus leaves its bankside burrow.

One of the strangest river animals is the platypus of Australia. It has a beak, webbed feet and lays eggs, like a duck. But it's not a bird, it's a monotreme – an unusual type of mammal. The platypus lives in the rivers and creeks of north and east Australia, poking and probing in the mud with its sensitive, leathery beak for worms, shellfish and other food.

Mississippi: blue catfish; **Ganges:** mugger crocodile; **Huang He:** river fox.

Spirits of the River

Even during the Stone Age, people lived near streams and rivers. They used the water for drinking, cooking and washing away waste. Rivers also provided fish, shellfish and other foods. Plants, such as reeds and rushes, became thatched roofs, mats, beds, cloaks and similar items. And the river was a barrier against dangerous animals or invading enemies – especially if you had a boat, and they did not!

Ritual cleansing

Many early peoples realized that they depended on rivers. So they made offerings to the gods and spirits of the waters. For centuries, the River Ganges has been holy to those who follow the Hindu faith – which includes four-fifths of the people in India. The Ganges' ever-flowing water is the symbol of life without end.

Flowers for the dead

People also go as pilgrims to the sacred Ganges city of Varanasi. It is a holy place to die. The bodies are burned or cremated, and the ashes scattered onto the waters, with bright marigold flowers. This ceremony helps the person to be reborn in another life.

Every day, pilgrims wash themselves in a traditional way in the Ganges to cleanse their souls.

Explorers: **Amazon:** Francisco de Orellana, 1541; **Mississippi:** Hernando de Soto, 1541

Rivers running through

Rivers feature in many other faiths and religions. Among the many gods of Ancient Greece were naiads, mystical spirits of rivers and lakes. In the Bible, baby Moses was found in a basket, hidden among the reeds and rushes of the Nile. An ancient Norse myth from Scandinavia tells how, before the Earth was created, eleven rivers flowed from a great well in the World of Death.

The Nile was of great importance to the Ancient Egyptians. It provided water for the crops that fed their great civilization for hundreds of years.

Heavenly bodies

The Nile was the life-blood of Ancient Egyptian civilization. Its regular floods brought fertile soil and moisture to feed their crops and it provided their main means of travel and transport. So it seemed natural for many Ancient Egyptians to believe that their sun-god, Re-Atum, journeyed across the sky each day in a boat. And that the moon and the stars travelled across the heavens in ships.

Early civilizations

By 5,000 years ago, Sumerian people farmed the land called Mesopotamia (modern Iraq). It was a "fertile crescent" between the Rivers Tigris and Euphrates. Crops grew well in the rich soil, watered by the rivers. People had time to devise new skills – such as writing and sculpture. They organized themselves into states centred on cities, and built huge palaces and temples for their rulers and priests. Their god Enki, "Lord of the Soil", was responsible for the rivers, rains and marshes.

A great feast in ancient Sumeria, carved in about 2,500 BC.

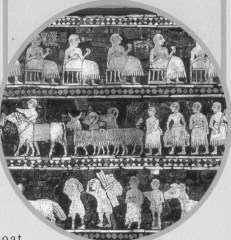

Nile: Pedro Paez (Blue Nile) in 1613, John Speke (White Nile) in 1860.

Water of Life

As ancient peoples settled in greater numbers, rivers became more important. About 5,000 years ago early Chinese civilizations grew up along the Huang He. Today the river irrigates 20 million hectares of fertile farmland for 100 million people. Other great civilizations grew up along rivers in India, the Middle East and North Africa.

Fertile soils

Over millions of years of floods and changes of course, the Huang He has laid down rich soils on the North China Plain. The mild climate allows farmers to grow crops such as wheat, rice, cotton and tea, with two or even three harvests a year. Most farmers still use traditional methods, with bullocks to pull ploughs and carts.

Growing rice in paddies depends on a plentiful supply of water.

2,500 years ago, the Chinese began to dig a canal for transport and irrigation. Its 1,780 kilometres took nearly 200 years to build.

Irrigating the fields

All crops need water – especially rice. It grows only in paddies – fields which are completely flooded. The water comes from the Huang He along specially built irrigation channels, some more than 2,000 years old. But it must be lifted into these channels by water-wheels or swinging buckets. The channels are also home to fish such as grass carp, which provide additional food.

Crops: **Amazon:** coffee, tropical hardwoods; **Nile:** cotton, corn, sugarcane;

This Chinese water-wheel, built from bamboo and wood, uses the river's own flow to lift its water up into irrigation pipes, to water the surrounding fields.

Major port

The Huang He is mostly shallow, and ice-covered in winter. It is not a main transport route, but it has several port-cities along its banks where local goods and produce are brought by trucks, carts and small boats, and loaded onto big ships for export. The banks and the river itself are used for markets.

Depending on the river

Two-thirds of the people in Congo (Zaire) are farmers. They depend on the huge, 4,650-kilometre-long Congo (Zaire) River and its hundreds of tributaries for almost everything. It is used for washing, bathing, drinking, irrigating fields of crops and watering animals. One of their main foods is river fish. Their main route for carrying produce and trading is – yes, the river.

Local rivers around the world can provide water for washing, drinking, cooking and fishing.

Many riverside towns have floating markets, like this one in Thailand.

Mississippi: cotton, soybean; **Ganges:** grains, cotton; **Huang He:** rice, wheat.

Floating Down the Highway

Rivers have always been useful for travel, transport, trade and exploration. The first river craft were probably simple rush or log rafts, pulled by ropes, or pushed by poles that became oars.

River to sea

At first, river travel was tiring – at least, going upstream was, with paddles or oars. The Ancient Egyptians were probably first to catch the wind with sails on boats, as they travelled the Nile 5,000 years ago. They built large vessels to carry giant stone blocks from the Upper Nile quarries to their pyramids and temples downstream. Soon riverboats were venturing out into the open sea, carrying goods for trade – and armies for conquest.

Traditional Arab vessels, dhows, still throng the Nile.

The world's longest waterway for boats links Canada's Mackenzie River to the USA's Mississippi. It uses rivers, lakes and canals along its 10,682 kilometres.

Exploration

Sailing ships carried traders and explorers across seas, and up the rivers of newly discovered continents. Southern and central North America were opened up as French pioneers explored the Mississippi from the north and south in the 17th century. Settlers followed close behind.

River ports (millions of people): **Nile:** Cairo (14); **Mississippi:** New Orleans (1.3);

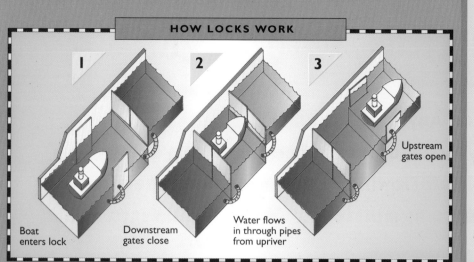

1

2

3

Upstream
gates open

Boat
enters lock

Downstream
gates close

Water flows
in through pipes
from upriver

Locks on canals allow boats to go
"uphill". Gates separate low water
from high water sections.

Tried and tested design

There are more boats on the
Chang Jiang (Yangtze) than on
all other rivers in China added
together. They vary from small
family craft to huge ocean-
going ships. Many are the
traditional junk design, but
modern engine-powered craft
also crowd the river.

Powerful tugs pull huge river
barges, like a locomotive on land
hauling a railway train.

First steamboat

In the early 1800s, engineers
developed steam-driven craft.
The engine turned a paddle
wheel on each side, and a flat
base prevented grounding. The
first of the famous Mississippi
steamboats was *New Orleans*,
in 1811. Twenty years later
there were 200 on the river.

A Mississippi rear paddle-steamer.

Modern river traffic

Steamboats carried passengers, freight, cowboys, musicians and gamblers through the
American Wild West. Today's Mississippi, like hundreds of other rivers around the world, is
still a vital highway. Besides great cargo ships that will head out across the seas, it has some
8,000 river tugboats, towing goods ranging from grain to petrochemicals, in long lines of
giant barges.

Amazon: Manaus (1); **Ganges:** Allahabad (1); **Huang He:** Kaifeng (0.5).

Factories and Industries

Rivers are moving water. Anything that moves has a type of energy. About 2,000 years ago people harnessed this energy by inventing the water-wheel. Flowing water pushes the wheel around and turns machinery, such as millstones, to grind grain into flour.

The largest water-wheel ever was built in Roman times, in Syria, to grind wheat. Called Mohammadieh Noria, it was 40 metres across.

Factories by the river

At the beginning of the Industrial Revolution, in the late 1700s, water-wheels powered factory machines for spinning and weaving. Soon steam engines replaced water power. But factories were still built on river-banks, using water to cool the equipment or to boil into steam. Boats brought fuels such as coal, and took away factory products.

Many power stations are by rivers and estuaries, so that they have a plentiful supply of cooling water.

Hydroelectricity

River power has been revived as hydro-electricity – "electricity from water". A dam is built across the river, and the water is channelled over huge fan-like turbine blades, making them turn generators, which produce electricity. It works best with fast rivers in narrow valleys.

Hydroelectricity makes it possible to generate electricity without burning fossil fuels such as coal, oil and gas. This saves resources and reduces pollution. Norway, Brazil and Congo (Zaire) make more than nine-tenths of their electricity in this way.

Industries: **Amazon:** minerals, timber; **Nile:** farming, fishing; **Huang He:** farming;

Glen Canyon hydroelectric dam, on the Colorado River, USA.

Mining by the River

The Rio Grande flows from the Rocky Mountains and forms the border between Texas, USA, and Mexico. Along its banks are mines for silver, gypsum (for cement and plaster) and potash (for fertilizer). But better known are its resources of oil and gas. Texas is famed for its oil wealth, and has nine-tenths of America's fossil fuel reserves.

River resources

Over millions of years, huge rivers deposit layer upon layer of sediment. The great weight of these layers presses on layers beneath, which harden and cement into rock. Under these conditions, rocks rich in coal, natural gas and oil may form.

The Amazon region is rich in metal ores – nickel, copper, tin, iron and manganese. Near the river's mouth are huge mines for bauxite, the ore from which aluminium is obtained. Meanwhile far upstream hopeful prospectors, knee-deep in mud, pan the Amazon for specks of gold.

The floating harbour and huge industrial city of Manaus is near the junction of the Amazon and the Rio Negro, "Black River".

Mississippi: manufacturing, farming; **Ganges:** farming, manufacturing.

Preserving Rivers

As people settled near rivers the water was a sewer for their body wastes and a dustbin for their rubbish. In ancient times, with fewer people, rivers could cope. But today, with billions of humans, factories, refineries and industries – our rivers are in trouble.

In many regions, rivers have become slow-flowing open sewers and rubbish dumps. This is Bangkok, Thailand.

From homes, factories and farms

Calcutta is India's second biggest city, with 11 million people. It grew up on the delta of the Ganges and Brahmaputra rivers. The waters became polluted with all manner of waste. People threw in sewage and trash from their homes. Factories poured in poisonous chemicals from processes such as leather tanning and cotton dyeing. Farmers nearby used artificial fertilizers that drained through the soil, into the river. The waters became dirty and smelly.

Threats: **Amazon:** logging; **Nile:** hydroelectric dams; **Mississippi:** bank erosion;

Clean it up!

This massive pollution made the Ganges one of the world's dirtiest rivers. It teemed with germs that cause cholera, typhoid, dysentery and other diseases. In 1985 the authorities began a huge clean-up campaign. They made new laws and built new sewage treatment works, with the aim of reducing the pollution by three-quarters.

Factory poisons pollute many rivers, killing fish and wildlife.

Egypt's Lake Nasser formed when the Aswan High Dam was completed across the Nile in the 1970s. It is 560 kilometres long.

More problems

At last, hundreds of rivers around the world are being cleaned up, like the Ganges. But there are other problems, too. Boats damage river-banks and leave oil trails in the water. Dams for hydroelectricity and irrigation form lakes that drown vast areas of land, including people's homes, and rare plants and animals. They also block fish like salmon and sturgeon, which need to swim upstream to breed. And they "steal" water and fertile sediments from farmlands far downstream. Some scientists suggest that earthquakes are triggered by the extra weight of water in lakes behind dams.

We must use our precious rivers with much greater care, so we can save their waters and wildlife for the future.

The Itaipu Dam on the Paraná River, between Paraguay and Brazil, is the world's largest hydroelectric scheme. It generates more than 13,000 million watts of electricity. But like many dams, it traps mud and sediments upstream. So the plains downstream no longer receive their nutritious helping of silt in the flood season. In many hydroelectric power stations, a portion of the electricity must be used to make artificial fertilizers, to replace the natural, fertile silt held back by the dam!

Each pollution incident damages our rivers further.

Ganges: flooding, pollution; **Huang He:** flooding, water diverted for irrigation.

Glossary

basin A generally bowl-shaped area of landscape, with the land sloping from high around the edges to low nearer the middle, where water runs and seeps and collects into a river or river system. *See also* watershed.

canyon A large gorge. *See also* gorge.

cataract A major stretch of fast-flowing water, which can include one or more waterfalls and rapids.

channel A long, narrow, valley-like area filled with running water, like a river channel, or a sea channel between close coastlines.

current Water flowing steadily in a particular direction, like the flow of a river.

delta An area of low-lying land at a river's mouth, made up of sediment deposited by the river.

drainage When water and other liquids seep and flow and run, pulled by gravity, often along a pattern of waterways.

erosion Gradual breaking down and wearing away of the land.

estuary The place where a river ends – its lower end or mouth, and where it widens and flows into the sea. Because of tides, the water is partly salty.

evaporate When a liquid turns into a gas or vapour. Often due to the heat of the Sun.

fertile For soils, those with plenty of nutrients and enough water to grow lots of plants, which could be natural, or farmed crops.

fossil fuel Prehistoric plants and animals that turned to fossils over millions of years, and which we now use as sources of energy. The main ones are coal, oil (crude petroleum) and natural gas.

gorge A narrow, deep valley with steep, cliff-like sides, which is usually smaller than a canyon.

granite Very hard type of rock, formed when liquid rock cools slowly and solidifies beneath the surface of the Earth.

irrigation Providing water, usually for plants to grow. It can be a natural process or man-made, as by water-wheels, pumps, ditches and pipes.

meander A curve in the course of a river, created as the river loses energy and slows due to the flattening of the land.

minerals Natural substances, sometimes formed as crystals, which make up the Earth's rocks. There are more than 3,000 types.

nutrients The essential substances that living things need to stay alive, grow, maintain and repair their bodies, and keep healthy.

ore Rocks and rocky materials that are rich in useful substances, like metals such as iron, gold or copper, or minerals such as sulphur.

plain A large area of relatively flat, smooth land. Dry plains are covered by grasses, while wet areas contain forests and swamps.

rapids On a river, a stretch of fast-flowing, shallow water.

rot To decay or decompose or break down naturally, like garden compost, and return to the soil.

sand bar A fairly long, narrow hump of sand, usually near the edge of a river, lake or sea, which may stick above the water's surface.

sediment Particles of rocks, stones silt, mud and dust that are carried along by moving water, and then fall or settle on the river or sea bottom when the flow slows or stops.

silt A substance formed from billions of tiny particles of rocks and minerals, and water. The particles are smaller than grains of sand.

source The place where a river starts – its upper end.

tributary A small side-branch of a river that flows into the larger main river.

tropical In the belt of land and sea around the Earth's middle, to either side of the Equator, where the climate is generally hot.

watershed The boundary line, or divide, between the headwaters of two separate river systems or basins.

Fact File

The world's ten longest rivers

NAME	LOCATION	FLOWS INTO	LENGTH (KM)
Nile	North-east Africa	Mediterranean Sea	6,670
Amazon	South America	South Atlantic Ocean	6,450
Chiang Jiang (Yangtze)	China	East China Sea	5,950
Huang He (Yellow)	China	Yellow Sea	4,830
Congo (Zaire)	Africa	South Atlantic Ocean	4,650
Missouri	Central USA	Mississippi/Missouri	4,350
Lena	Northern Asia	Arctic Ocean	4,250
Niger	West Africa	South Atlantic Ocean	4,200
Mekong	South-east Asia	South China Sea	4,180
Yenisey	Northern Asia	Arctic Ocean	4,100

The world's five biggest rivers by volume of water flowing in them

NAME	LOCATION	FLOWS INTO	FLOW
Amazon	South America	South Atlantic Ocean	180,000
Congo (Zaire)	Africa	South Atlantic Ocean	40,000
Chang Jiang (Yangtze)	China	East China Sea	34,000
Paraná	South America	South Atlantic Ocean	22,000
Orinoco	South America	Caribbean-Atlantic	20,000

Flow is in cubic metres per second into the sea. An average school classroom is 200 cubic metres.

Five famous cities and their rivers

CITY/COUNTRY	RIVER NAME	LENGTH (km)
Paris, France	Seine	776
New York City, USA	Hudson	510
London, England	Thames	260
Tokyo, Japan	Sumida	45
Sydney, Australia	Parramatta	30

The Valentre bridge (above) spans the Lot River in Cahors, France.

Some major river bridges

(many famous big bridges are across sea inlets, bays, large estuaries or straits between islands)

NAME	RIVER/CITY/COUNTRY	BRIDGE TYPE	LENGTH (metres)
George Washington	Hudson, New York, USA	Suspension	1067
Bendorf	Rhine, Coblenz, Germany	Cement girder	1031
Salazar	Tagus, Lisbon, Portugal	Suspension	1014
Pont de Quebec	St Lawrence, Quebec, Canada	Cantilever truss	987
Pont du Normandie	Seine, Le Havre, France	Cable-stayed	856
Port Mann	Fraser, British Columbia, Canada	Arch	366
Lower Yarra	Yarra, Melbourne, Australia	Cable-stayed	336

Index

Africa 5, 10, 14, 17, 18, 22
Alaknanda River 6
Amazon, River 4, 5, 6, 9, 12, 14,
    16, 17, 18, 20, 22, 24, 26, 27,
    28
Andes Mountains 4, 6, 7
animals 16, 17, 18-19, 29
Arizona 9
Australia 13, 19

Bangladesh 7, 13, 15, 26
Bhagirathi River 6
birds 18, 19
Brahmaputra River 7, 13, 15, 28
Brazil 11, 13, 29

Calcutta 28
Canada 11
canals 5, 22, 30
canyons 8; see also Grand
    Canyon
cataracts 10, 11, 30
China 5, 12, 13, 22, 23
Colombia 7
Colorado River 9, 27
Columbus, Christopher 7
Congo River 23
cotton 22, 23
crocodiles 19
crops 21, 22

dams 9, 26, 27, 28, 29
deltas 7, 14, 15, 28, 30
deserts 5, 10, 14

Earth 9, 11, 21
earthquakes 29
Egyptians, Ancient 5, 21, 24
erosion 8, 9
estuaries 14, 15, 30
Euphrates, River 21

farming 5, 13, 21, 22, 23, 26, 27
first-order streams 6
fish 17, 18, 19, 20, 22, 23, 26, 29
floods 9, 12, 13, 15, 19, 22
food 20, 22
fossil fuel 26, 27, 30

Ganges, River 5, 6, 8, 13, 15, 17,
    19, 20, 23, 25, 27, 28, 29
glaciers 8
gorges 8, 11, 16, 30
Grand Canyon 9

Himalaya Mountains 6, 7
Hindus 5, 6, 7, 20
hippos 18
Huang He River 5, 7, 9, 10, 12,
    13, 15, 17, 19, 22, 23, 25, 26,
    27
hydroelectricity 26, 27, 28, 29

India 5, 7, 13, 15, 20, 22, 28
Indus River 7
industry 26-27, 28
irrigation 22, 23, 29, 30

Mars 5
meanders 8, 10, 13, 30
metals 27
Mexico 27
    Gulf of 15
Minnesota 7
Mississippi River 5, 7, 8, 13, 14,
    15, 17, 19, 20, 23, 24, 25, 27

Nanda Devi 6, 7
Niagara Falls 11
Niagara River 11
Nile, River 5, 6, 9, 10, 11, 13, 15,
    16, 17, 18, 19, 20, 23, 24, 26,
    28

Okavango River 14, 16
Orinoco River 7
ox-bows 13

Paraná River 29
plants 16-17, 18, 20, 29
pollution 28-29

rainforest 7, 16
rapids 10, 30
religion 5, 20-21
rice 22, 23
Rio Grande 27
Rio Negro 13, 27
river basins 4, 12

second-order streams 6
sediment 9, 14, 29, 30
shellfish 18, 19, 20
silt 5, 12, 14, 15, 30
South America 5, 7

Thailand 23, 28
Thames, River 15
Tigris, River 21
transport 5, 23, 24-25
tributaries 4, 6, 7, 11, 16, 23, 30

USA 11, 27

water cycle 7
waterfalls 11
water hyacinths 17
water lilies 16, 18, 19
water-wheels 23, 26
wheat 22, 23

Yellow River see Huang He
Yellow Sea 12

Zaire River 23